MISSION: WEIRD WEATHER

SHINOY AND THE CHAOS CREW

Written by Chris Callaghan

Illustrated by Amit Tayal

Collins

When Shinoy downloads the Chaos Crew app on his phone, a glitch in the system gives him the power to summon his TV heroes into his world.

With the team on board, Shinoy can figure out why weird things are happening in Flat Hill. Is the dastardly red-eyed S.N.A.I.R., a Super Nasty Artificial Intelligent Robot, causing all the trouble or is it something else?

Dad

Myra, Shinoy's sister

Mum

Shinoy

Toby, Shinoy's best friend

Milo

The CHAOS CREW

Ember

Merit

Salama

Bug

Lazlo

Mustang Harry

S.N.A.I.R.

It was just another morning in Flat Hill. Shinoy and Toby were teaching Milo some tricks.

That's it, Milo. Here's another treat.

He's good at spinning one way, but he won't spin the other!

Suddenly ...

Who turned the lights out?

?!?

Woof!

What's going on?

I'm sure it wasn't this dark five minutes ago!

3

4

There was only one thing to do …

Come on, chaos boy. Do your stuff.

Go on, press the app!

Call to Action –

Chaos Crew!

Back on Earth ...

Give us 12 hours and we'll move our planet out of your space. What could possibly go wrong?

Look at our shadows!

Something's not right about them.

And they're moving. Why are they moving?

Back home ...

It's getting crazy!

Earth is spinning faster than it should. And in the opposite direction to normal.

That explains the weird shadows!

There are going to be more weird effects.

Like what?

Like the sun setting where it usually rises.

Everything's happening in a back to front way!

The storm hits, but the Chaos Crew are ready.

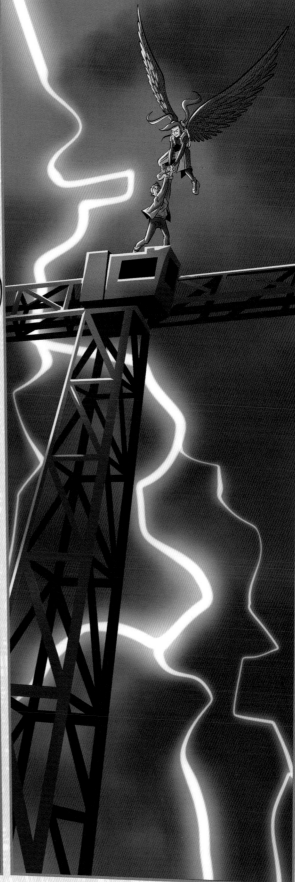

Sunrise over Flat Hill ...

The water level's dropping.

It was time for someone to have an idea.

I've got an idea. You have two moons now, ours and yours. And a whole new nearby planet – Earth!

Is that enough extra gravity?

Changing gravity supply settings.

One hour until full charge!

Yes!

The storm fades.

Your idea saved Earth. Impressive.

Your world is safe again.

But Further Earth is still stuck in a solar storm. Until next time, amigos!

Storms ahead

Today the sky will be full of a NEW PLANET.

Followed by darkness.

Strange shadows.

Chilly, howling winds.

And birds flying weirdly.

The Earth will rotate the wrong way.

Heavy rainfall will follow.

And more howling winds.

There will be storms.

And more storms.

Followed by a sunny spell.

Solar storms are still present in space.

 Ideas for reading

Written by Christine Whitney

Primary Literacy Consultant

Reading objectives:

- discuss the sequence of events in books
- make inferences on the basis of what is being said and done
- predict what might happen on the basis of what has been read so far

Spoken language objectives:

- ask relevant questions
- speculate, imagine and explore ideas through talk
- participate in discussions

Curriculum links: Science: Experience and observe phenomena; Writing: Write for different purposes

Word count: 784

Interest words: solar storm, planetary system, solar or wind power, gravity

Build a context for reading

- Challenge children to predict the story from its title, *Mission: Weird Weather*.
- Ask children to explain day and night. Support them in their understanding.
- Discuss the idea of solar and wind power. Ask if anyone has seen a wind farm.

Understand and apply reading strategies

- Read up to page 5 and ask children what problem Shinoy and his family are facing?
- Continue to read to page 12. On page 10, Bug says, *You may experience some side effects from Further Earth being so close to Earth*. Encourage children to reread the text and find the *side effects* Bug is talking about.
- Read to page 18. Ask children to explain Shinoy's idea for getting extra gravity power.
- Read to page 21. The storm has passed for Shinoy and his family, but what problem still faces the Chaos Crew?

Develop reading and language comprehension

- Read page 3 together. What word tells the reader that it shouldn't have been dark at that time?
- On page 16, Shinoy says, *So that's a no then?* Ask children to explain what he means by this.
- Discuss with children what could happen in another adventure for the Chaos Crew as Merit says, *But Further Earth is still stuck in a solar storm. Until next time, amigos!*
- Ask children to look at the illustrations on pages 22 and 23 and to talk about how they summarise what happened in Flat Hill that day.

Support a creative response

- Observe and record the weather near you for a week. You might try this at different times of the year.
- Imagine you are a news reporter for the Flat Hill Times. Write a short newspaper article about the strange effects of the weather that day in Flat Hill.
- Investigate alternative ways to create energy.

Read more

Mission: Static Shocks (Purple/Band 8) is a graphic novel in the Shinoy and the Chaos Crew series.